Residual Affects

Poetry and Pictures

Composed By

Erika Renee Land
KaTisha Smittick

Residual Affects Poetry

Erika Renee Land
www.erikarland.com

ISBN 978-0-9852836-2-9
LCCN: 2013957175

Residual Affects Photography

KaTisha J. Smittick
KSmittick@gmail.com

"Be kinder than necessary, because everyone is fighting some kind of battle."

--J.M. Barrie

Dedication

To my family

Parts of Me

Yin and Yang have been my saviors since my great departure from everything I once was.

The good and bad coexisting together within this Leo, covered by a darkened rainbow of stars.

The first I said I would call my love understood it all, even though we experienced an epic fall.

Lollipops and an alter ego have led me to be who I am today, much different from the soldier I once was.

The one you knew, young and catatonic emotionally, driving you to extremes of instability, has finally healed.

I want to say thank you for hanging in there and being a friend, when romance came to an end.

ERL

DEDICATED TO

Mina Smittick and Jered Davison

First and foremost, I want to thank God for giving me strength, courage, and a sound mind. I want to thank my family, friends and especially my cousins Mina and Jered who were more like siblings.

For Jered,

I've seen plenty of soldiers die and buried.
Twenty-one gun salutes, the lowering of caskets,

Listened to the roll calls where the soldier never answers.

I've always been strong throughout it all, Until the day I had to bury my cousin,
"The Soldier"- a piece of me. We have cried the same cries.

I am that soldier who sat next to you and helped you fight that battle.

I am that soldier who cried those cries for our fallen comrades,
But I never thought I'd be the soldier
That had to be the soldier
That watched a part of me, my family, a soldier die.

Today is that day, when I can truly say I've lost the soldier within me.
That 21 gun salute means more to me.
Those army values mean less to me,
This civilian life I'm living, now, has more value to me.

#RIP, my cousin, my fallen comrade, America's soldier. I salute you!!!

KJS

Responses
Evoked
By
Secret
Insecurities
Drafted
Unconsciously
After
Life

And
Failures
Forged
Erika's
Creative writing
And
Tai's
Subjective photography

Table of Contents

SOCIETAL AFFECTS

Changes in Thinking
Not
Emotional Responses

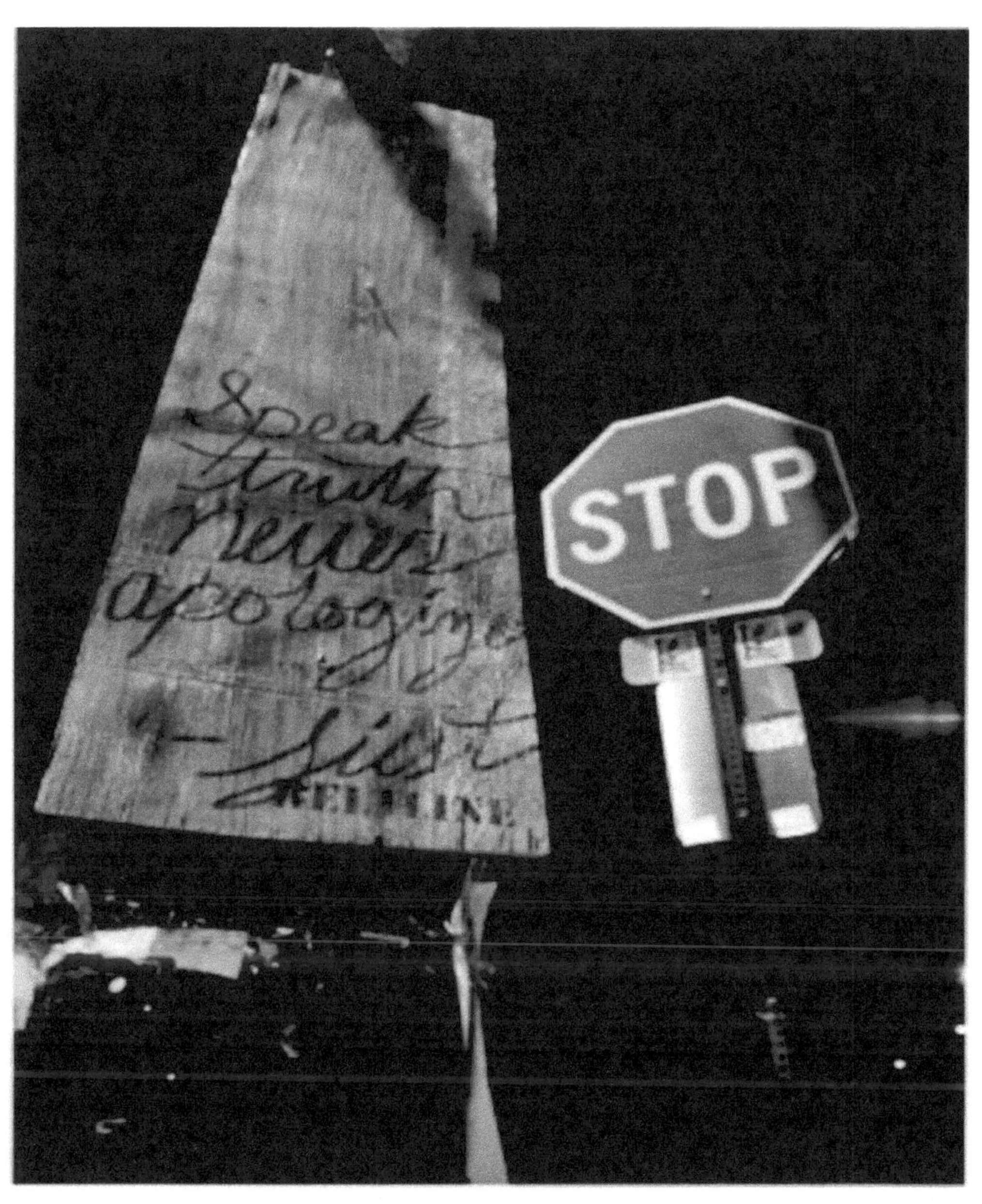

Stop and Pay Attention

Michael Jackson

Yesterday, I cried for a man I barely even knew.
Radio broadcasts, camera lenses, magazines, and
TV screens are what I got to know him through.
But, through those means, I was able to form a dense being.

Many never got to know his true character,
Though he appeared to be a true, kind, gentle fellow,
We discussed, degraded, and berated him as a caretaker.
And he took what was dished and always stayed mellow.

From the outside in, it seems one who had it all lost it all. Most of us
looked past the great tragedy of his life
As we sat back laughing and watching his great fall, Pondering
our lives if granted that golden knife.

Many times, we laughed at the greatest entertainer of all time, While all he
wanted to do was be like you and I,
And sleep for eight hours at a time.

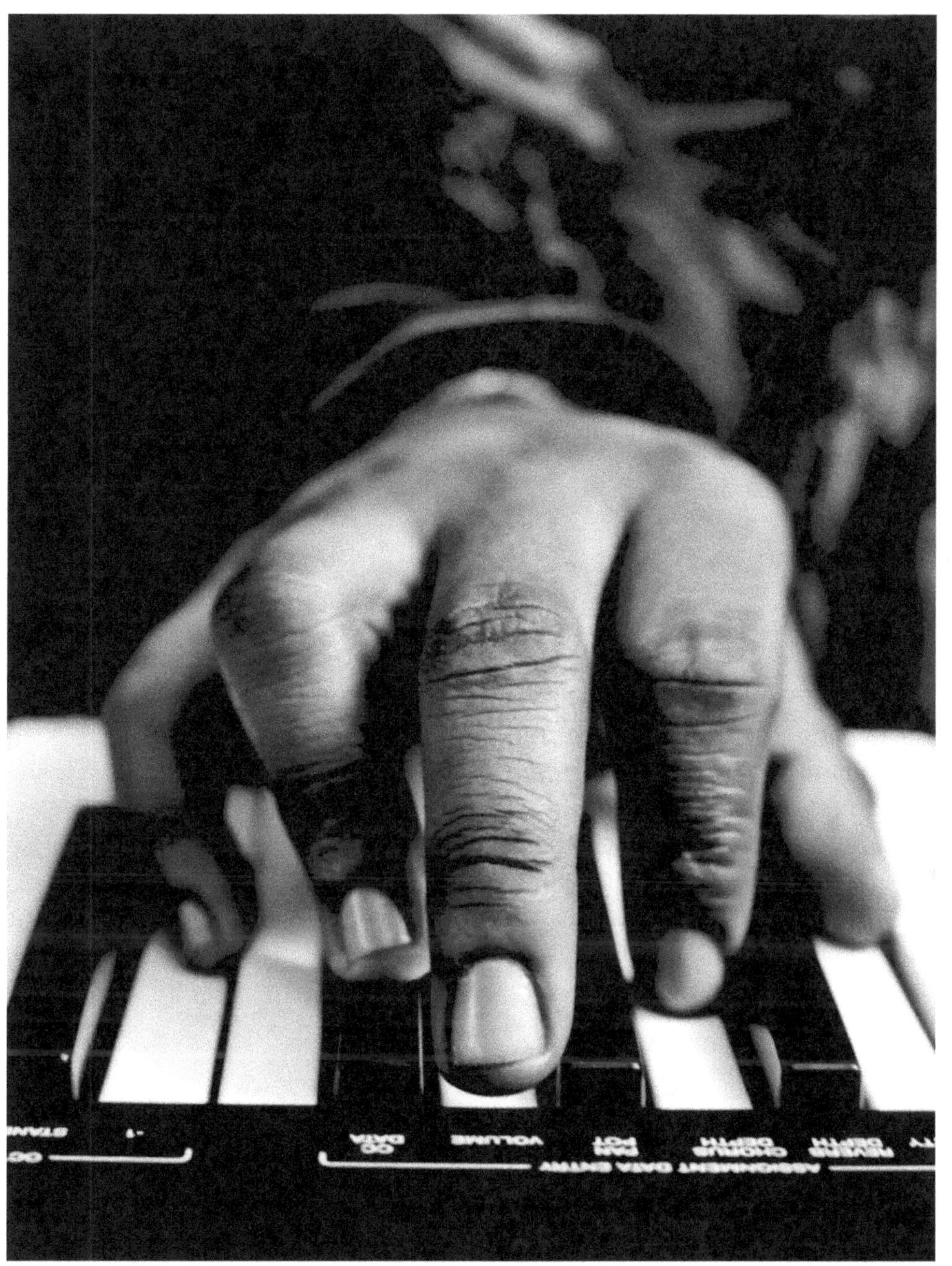

Music Fingers

Fusing the Pieces

The sun is dying.
Love never ceases.
Time never ends.

A cyclical relationship:
Hoping, yearning, and wanting.
Watching, waiting, and wondering.

Burning a hole in me.
The clock has stopped,
Causing love to die.

I am imploding.
I am done.
It is over.

The sun is dying, and I am imploding.
This cyclical relationship is burning a hole in me.
Love never ceases, but this hoping, yearning, and wanting is causing my love to die.
Time never ends, but it took too long.
The watching, waiting, and wondering has caused the clock to stop.

Finally is it over, I am done with the pain.

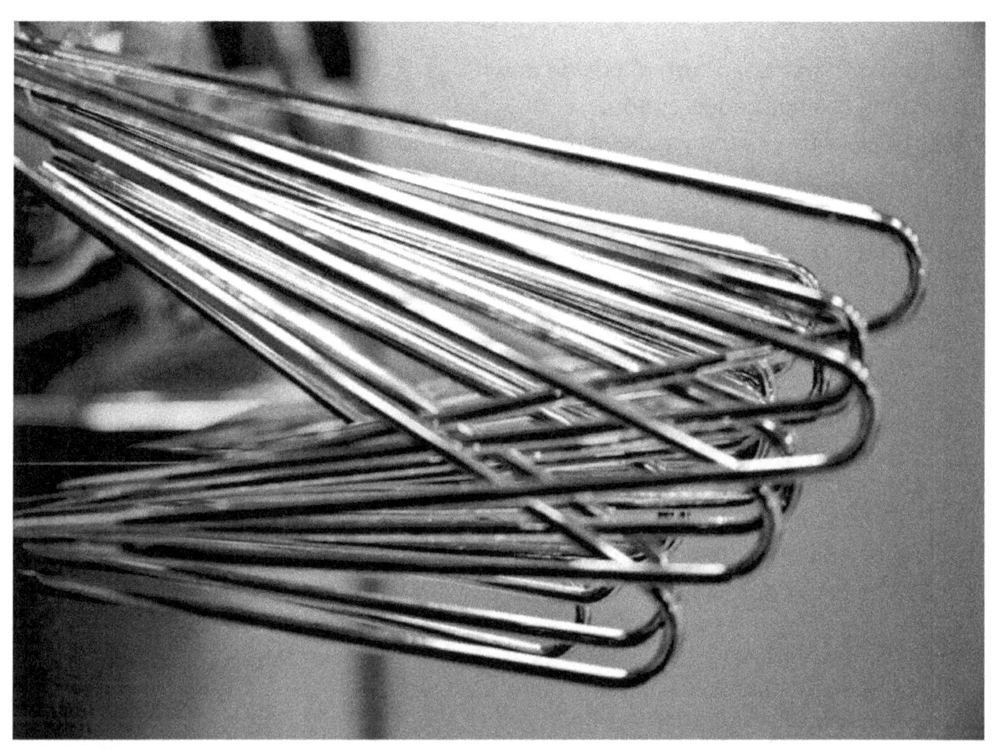

Entangled

You Remind Me

You remind me of a rock dropped in water, displacing everything around you.

You've moved me, unraveled me, stripped me emotionally, crippled me mentally, ravished my heart with the pushing and pulling.

My world has been turned upside down,
Yet nothing has happened to you.
Through all of this chaos you have remained unmoved.
There seems to be no compromise with you.

Through peering eyes, you set me on fire,

And I
Am losing
All my
Desire

My sense of self has been lost because of you.
Daily fronting because I only want to please you.
Maybe you really don't want my coos.
Maybe I am unmoving for wanting to be with you.

This is my fault for being so caught up in you.
Wait, no. I won't do it again, turn this into my personal issue.
See, like ripples in the sea, this is recurring for you,

Constantly you have thrown me away,
While I have continued to stay.

You remind me of a rock dropped in water, displacing everything around you,
but it won't happen to me again.

For today I am walking away, sweet nothings no longer will float toward you.

Only your own muffled sounds as you furiously drift around, and
then drown.

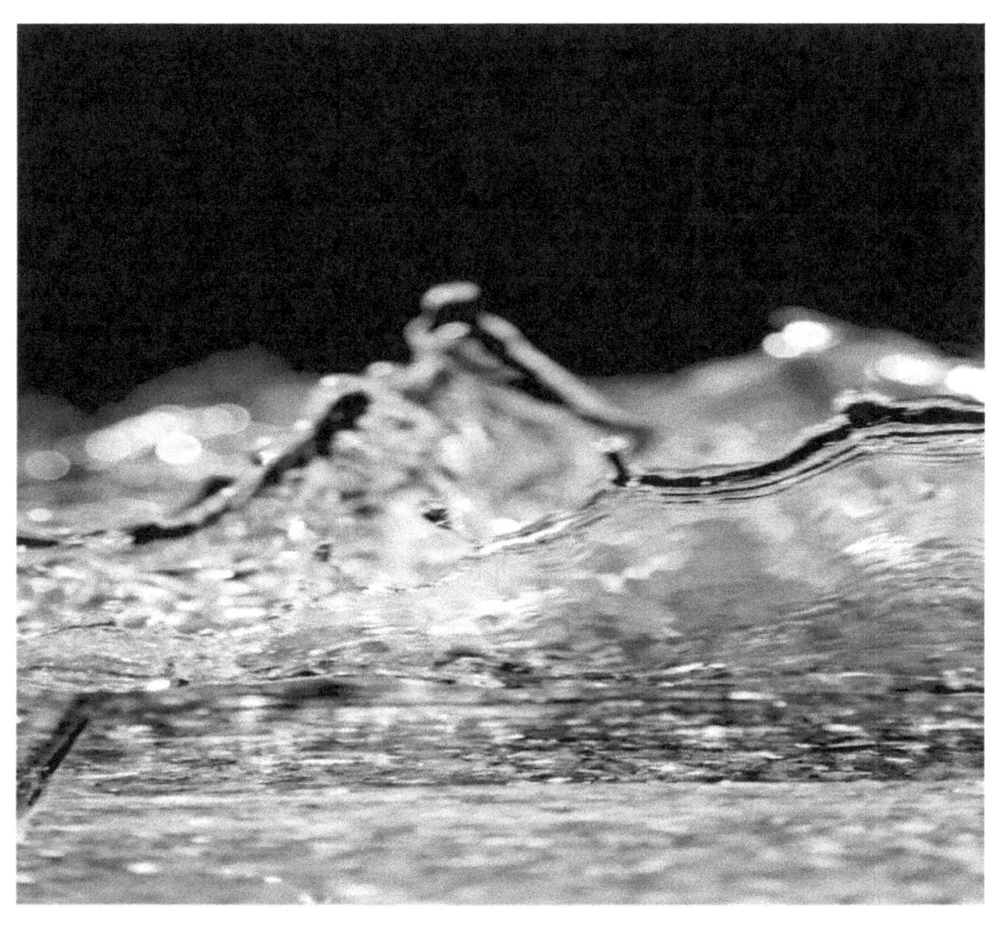

Splash

Repetitive Story

What he has been through,
I am going through,
And one day you will too.

Life is like a water wheel,
Shit gets picked up and thrown off the other side,
That same shit gets picked up again and thrown off the other side.

His life's experiences watered down by dripping water,
Filter through to be picked up by me differently,
Then along will come you to play in that same stream.

Why won't we learn to do things differently?

Passed along memories of his disasters
Have made me a master
Of the same things you will do faster,

Life is like a water wheel,
Shit gets picked up and thrown off the other side,
That same shit gets picked up again and thrown off the other side.

And after he is long gone
I will stand there and catch the dung,
Maybe one day my descendants will realize what is being flung.

Hopefully, they will do things differently, and change will finally come.

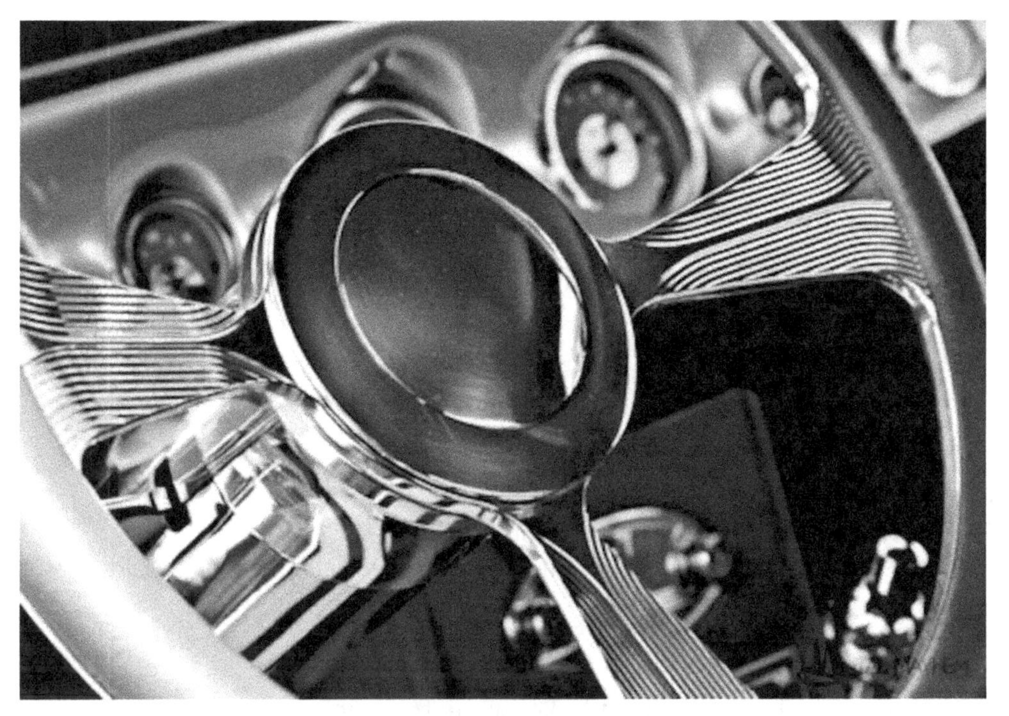

Repetitive Notions

Lost Identity

How can I be on the creep if you keep recognizing me?
I'm in this shit deep struggling to break free,
Blending and fading not wanting to be seen.

You criticize me, not for who I am, but who I chose to be. I criticize you, but who exactly are you?
We both wear these masks so no one know what's underneath.

How can I be on the creep if you keep recognizing me?
I'm blending and fading not wanting to be seen.

This mask I wear hides my true identity.
It's a harsh cruel world made tolerable for me.
By creating an alter ego, you see,
People are less cruel to me.

But here you are trying to make me find me.
Take off your mask and you'll see it's not that easy.
People pass judgment without understanding.
People tear you down while disregarding their own fallacies.

What I'm trying to say is

I wear a mask so no one will get to know the true me.
I wear a mask to hide who I am because it's much easier to get by.
I wear a mask because it's much easier when I'm criticized.
The problem is I have gotten so used to the fake me that I don't even know the real me.

I don't want to blend and fade into society anymore,
And one day I'll break free and finally get to know the true me,

But until then,

> How can I be on the creep if you keep recognizing me?
> Leave me alone to blend and fade and never be seen.

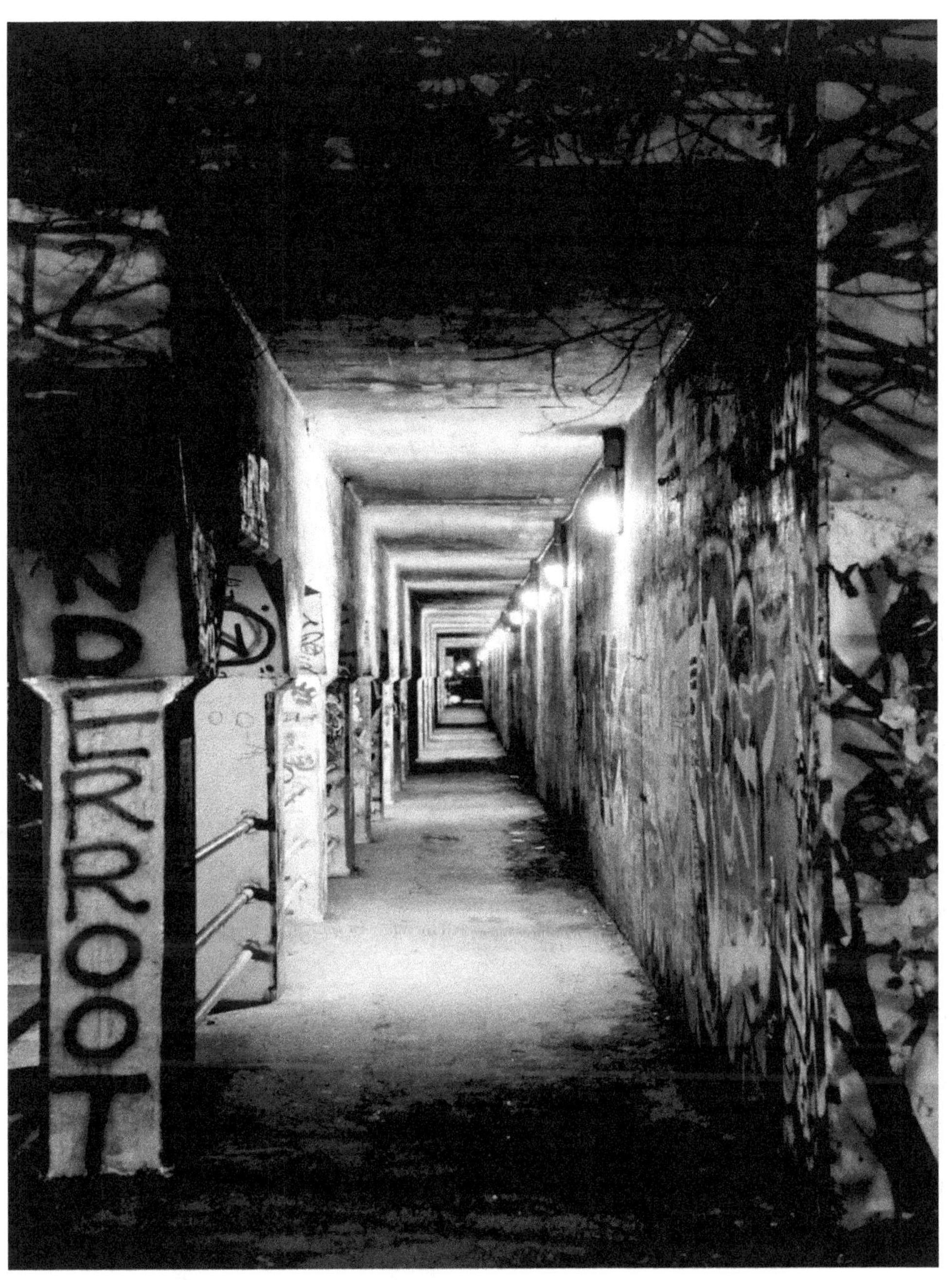

Pathways

Water Falls

When I wake up in the morning, I have to face myself.
All the wrongdoings, pain caused and suffered,
Are reflected back at me.
In the mirror, all that remains,
The sliver of myself lost out here in the trees.

I'm trying to be as free as the raindrops in the streams
Rushing over a steep rift,
To find the calm of the seven seas.
I can hear their screams—they are mine.

Out here in the trees, my sincerity is the deepest.
Here, the truest part of me lies,
Waiting to be resurrected.
All the hostility, exemplified by flashing cameras, Is looking for cessation.
I just want to be free to be me.
Let the genius in me take off toward futuristic things
I thought I'd never see.
Find a resting place after fleeing,
The torrential currents of my former strife.

I want to be free enough to chase myself.
As I find waterfalls below the equator,
Outside of the place that birthed me,
Then vilified me without knowing the conflicts that haunt me.

I want to be free,
Like the cold droplets from a waterfall,
Finding their place out there,
After free falling into tranquility.

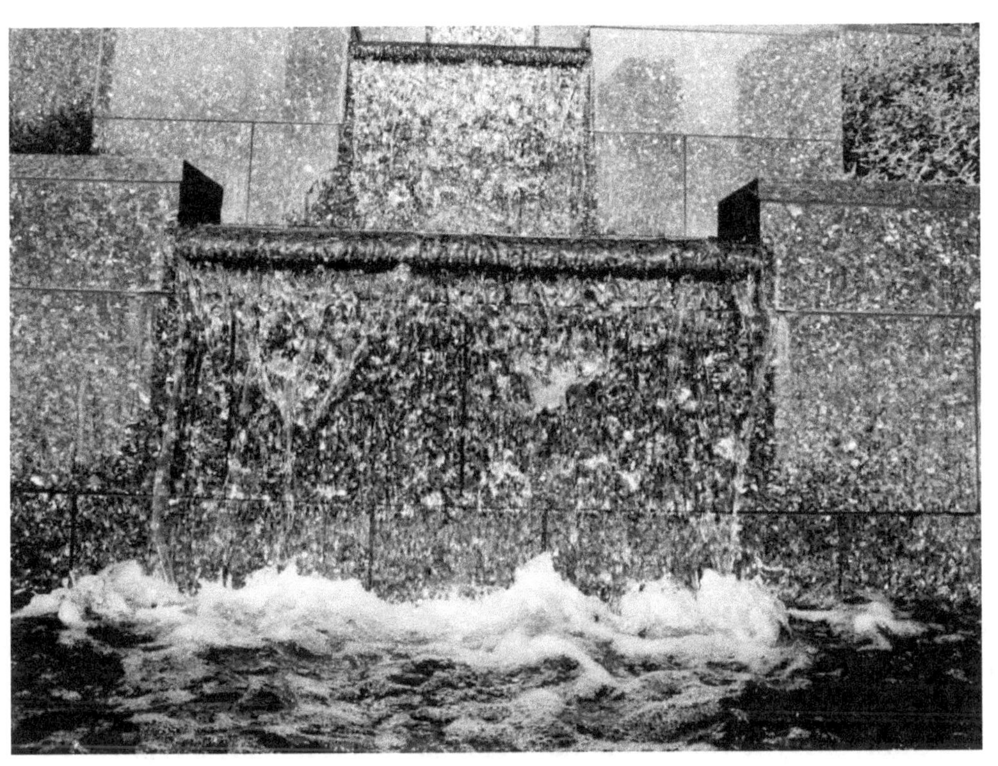

Falling Water

Pros V. Cons

Please, please, don't condemn me to those steel bars and stone walls.

Give me a chance at life to learn something.
Expand my heights above that treacherous wire.
Don't confine me in those walls.
Let my mind learn things, outside the box.
Don't hinder my intelligence by clouding it with spikey thoughts of how to make a dollar off that crack rock.

Let me peek out into the world, run my fingers through white sands, instead of crystal powders.
Scheming on all the things that will get me stuck behind those four walls, instead of how to legally make 15 out of one dollar -- *[Wall Street]*.

Why can't you send me to that place where
California in-state tuition cost two thousand less over four years, than a yearly out-of-state stay at an Arizona prison.

Touch beyond the Arizona skies is what I want to do.
Please don't stifle me over one hundred unpaid parking bills.

"Guilty! Maybe you should have thought about it being a crime."

Excuse me, your honor, may I please, please, make one last plea to null this straight-to-jail-do-not-pass-go you've handed me?

Professionally, I was not making it, busting my behind at that stupid 9 to 5.

Delivering newspapers, not during the night, but in the day, along with coffee to my nincompoop editor-in-chief who won't let me publish my stories because they don't involve kitties.

Your honor I plead, please send me back to school and I promise I'll get a useful degree studying something like economics. *Wait. Does that count? I mean Economist, we need them right?*

Because our economy is in travesty, which leads me again to the beginning of this plea. I got a degree, but my pay is low, so I couldn't pay the tickets.

But then again, it's the system, right?

Maybe I could have paid them if I hadn't gone to college and remained on the block hustling the hustlers, and well you fill in the blank. See, then I would have the money and wouldn't be here in front of you.

By imprisoning me, all I'll learn to do is rob and steal efficiently, instead of being in a seat, hand raised loudly, so I can contribute to this fucked up society.

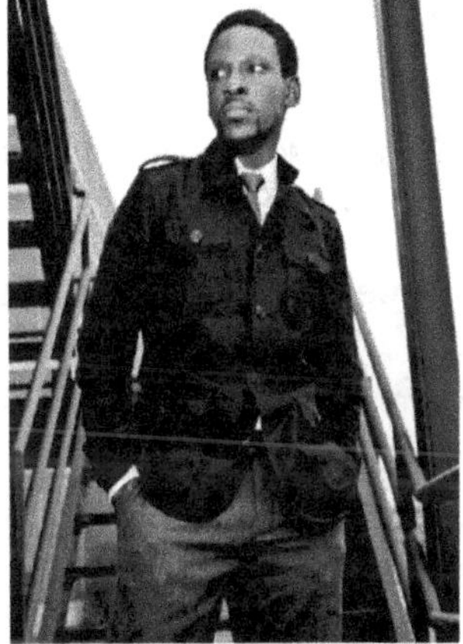

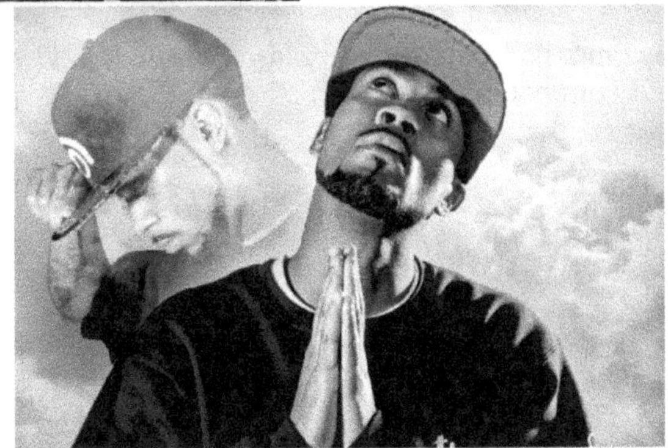

Tainted Honey Pots

- *inspired by* The Honey Launderers: Uncovering the Largest Food Fraud in U.S. History *by Susan Berfield*

The silver lining of the big picture that gets past us all.

Customs of customers expand way beyond the seven seas.
Our demands outfit the production of authenticity.

My goodness, what has the world come to?
When we see the error of our ways but turn a blind eye?
To feed that uncontrollable need to have a sweetness that's bitter in origin.

When will enough be enough here in America?
When will we not have to count on the Chinese
To bail our government out?

A faulty system exists in which the politicians can't pull up their bootstraps and help the constituents of the greatest country, where government shutdowns are imminent to prove unscientific theories of what the people want. When no one asked the people!

Please, let us go back to the time when we didn't have to rely on tainted honey pots.
Bailouts: one way or another, from a country we judge for not having more than two sons,
Where food is sometimes scarce and resources are significantly below the inhabitant total,
Because they are feeding an over-consuming country that, in turn, shuns their customs… Etcetera.

America should be ashamed to reject gallons of honey from the Chinese.
India's honey production can't keep up with world needs.
Tainted or not, where would we be if it weren't for the Chinese?

By laboring for ninety percent below their paid worth, they are helping to keep our commerce free.

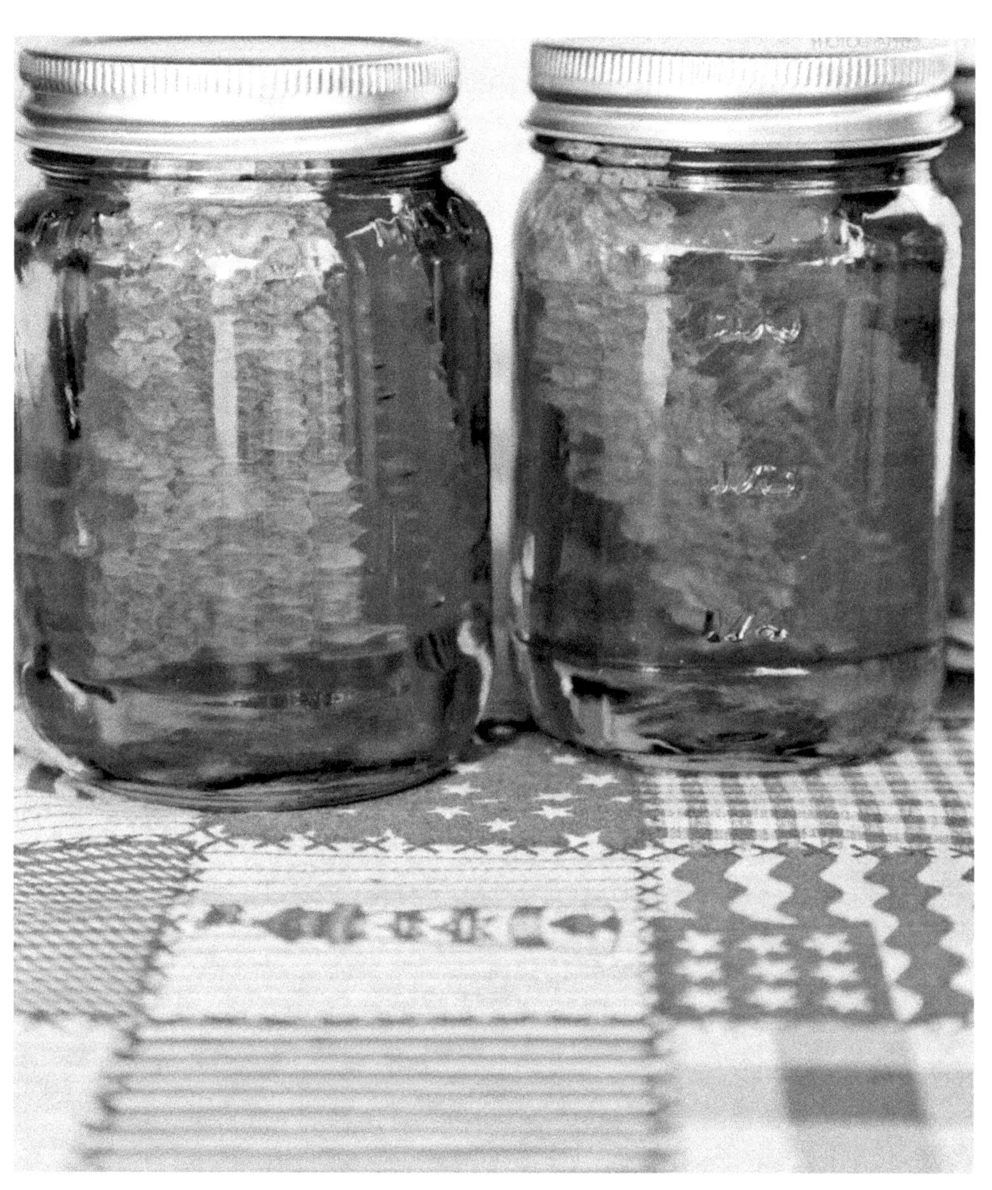

American Made Honey

WAR RESIDUALS

Unsung Heroes and Uncounted Casualties

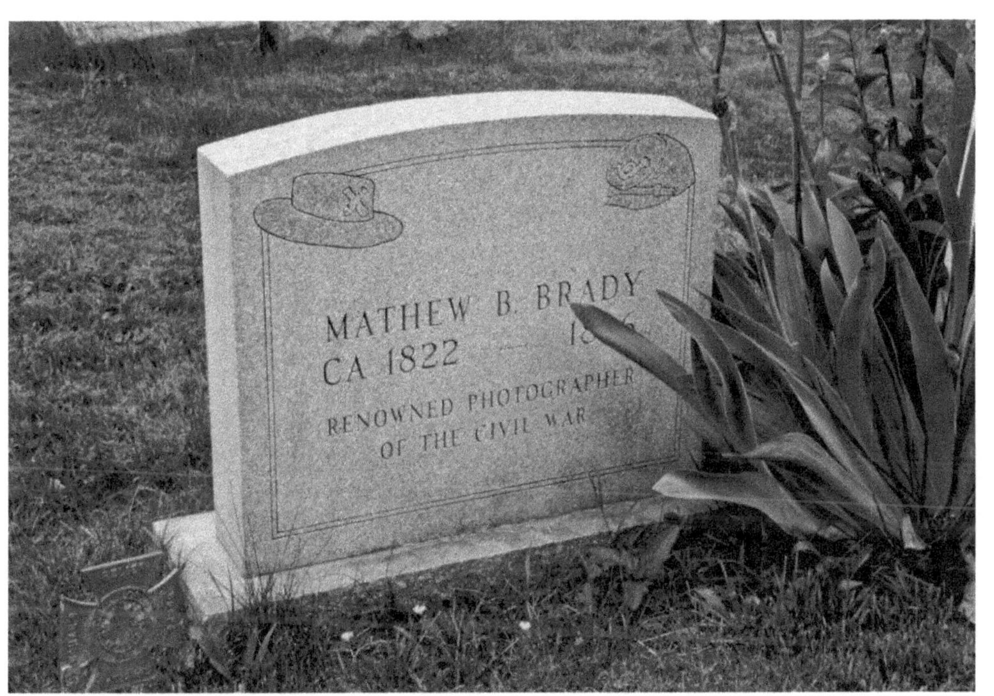

Fame After Death

Overdose

She had a seizure trying to cope Was it cocaine?
No. Was it weed? No
Was it ecstasy? No
What about heroin? Like in Vietnam? Nope

Benadryl often functions as dope out there in the desert
sands when soldiers are trying to cope with their
comrades dying in their hands.

Benadryl may not have been lethal that night, but she was a step away from David's fate—

He committed suicide.

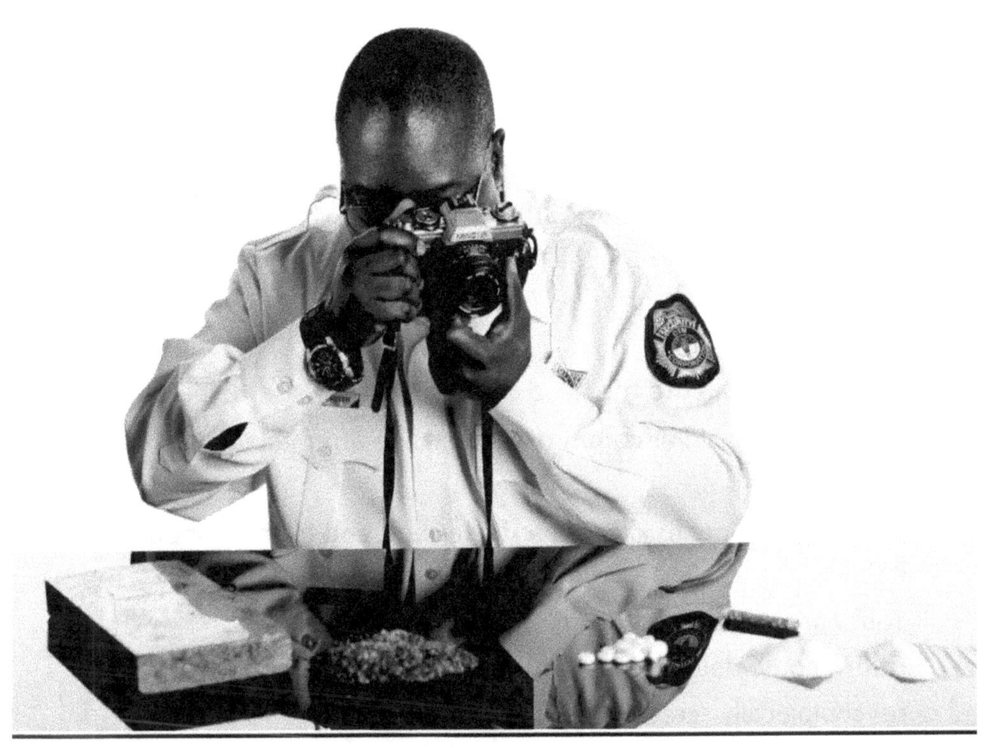

Illegally it feels good

Broken Soldiers

The army has a saying,
One shot, one kill.
And I fucking hate it,
Because that's all it took David to make himself still.

David risked his life but was met with nothing but strife from an ungrateful wife. And we lost one of the sweetest men known in the 47th CSH.

And while a bullet to the head may be bad,
Better than a soldier committing homicide after going mad.

Teaching soldiers to kill with a single shot, and to think about it not.

Youth are turned into killing robots Only to
return home devoid of emotion,
psychologically screwed
and then,
and then,
Killing sprees ensue.

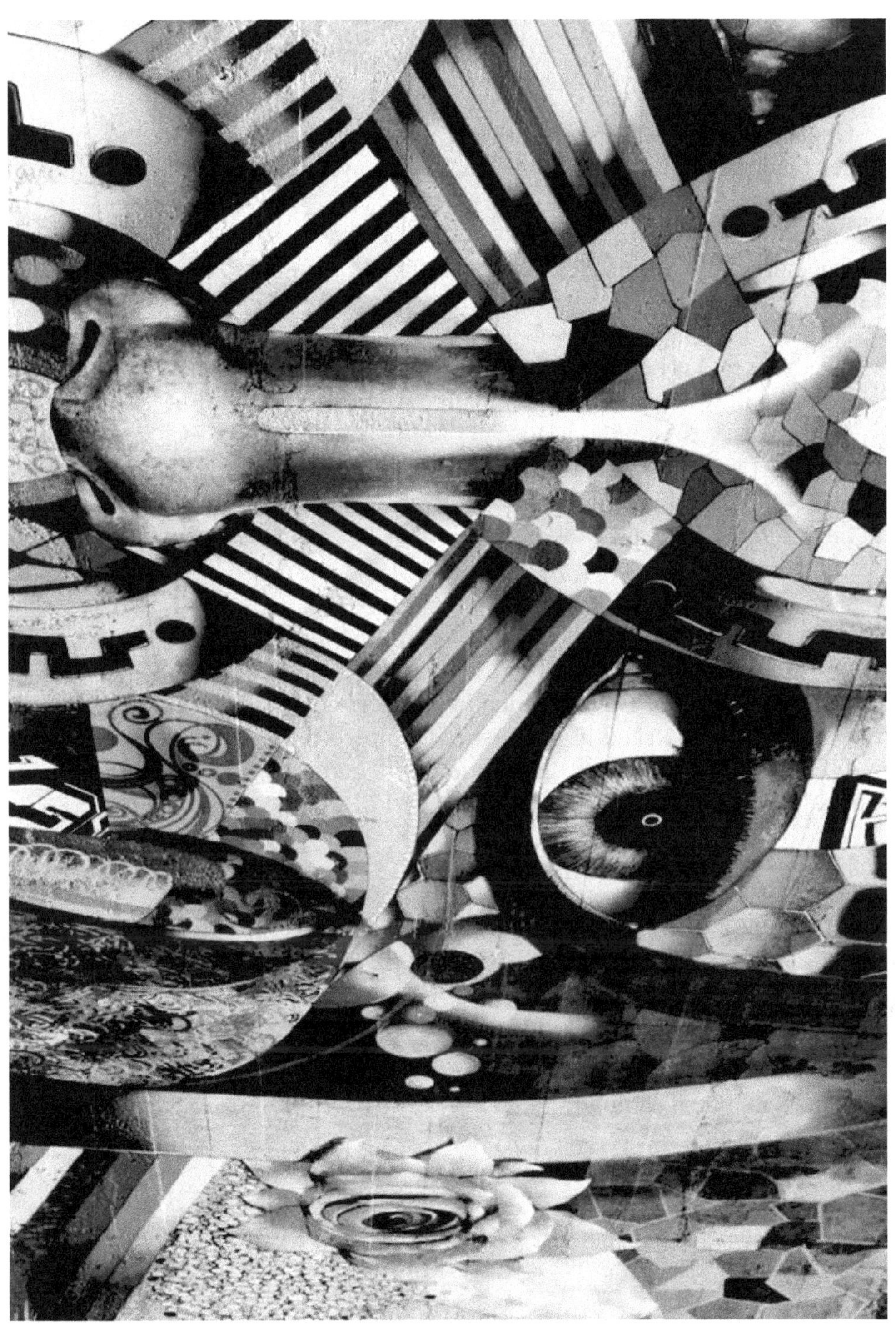

Adrenaline

One strike. Two strikes. The towers fall. The world is sad. He gets mad. We all get mad, but it's his shot to call. Where we will be when the adrenaline wears off?

One strike. Two countries. We must invade them all. To avenge the deaths of how many people? The total's always wrong.

His excuse. Our belief: weapons of mass destruction.
Where will we be when the adrenaline wears off?

Not one. Not two. Over ten years later, if you ask him, "Where are we with this war?" he'd probably simply say, "Right where we need to be." While he's out hunting deer with old Dick Cheney.

For him it has. For us it has not.
Someone tell me: when is the adrenaline going to wear off?

Not one. Not two. But three deployments later, and I can't fucking sleep at night, so I count the sand grains that have blown through the door, thinking to myself, When am I going to go home? Is it going to be when the adrenaline wears off?

It never fucking wears off!

Two people, one divorce. She doesn't understand that I have PTSD, so she left me, now I am all alone, someone tell me when is the adrenaline going to wear off.

Someone tell me when is the adrenaline going to wear off. I'm starring at the clouds, maybe it should right now.

One click: The war it's a piece of me now.

Two clicks: It has shattered my thoughts, and I can't piece them together again.

Three click: No matter how hard I try to push it away, I can't put it down. Man, the adrenaline sure is pumping now.

Fourth click: I can't let go of that man who starring me in the eye when I was letting him die.

BOOM.

Ascension to the clouds.

Finally, the adrenaline rush has calmed down.

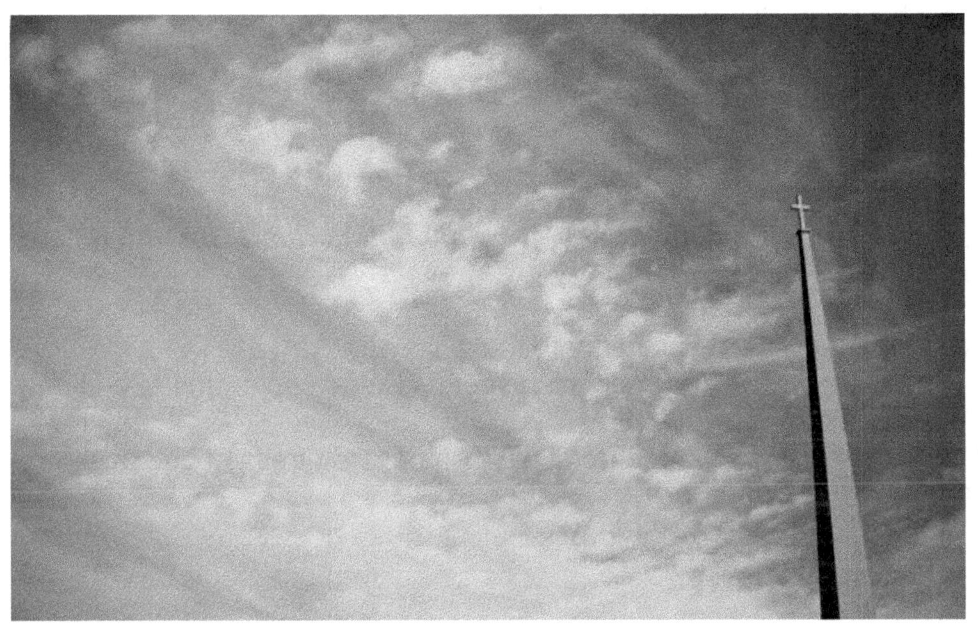

Look Up!

Ceiling Fans

These sand-grains hurt my face,
I can't put it down
The wind is so strong,
I can't put it down
I get lost in the choppers
I can't put it down
Let me go, I have to save them
I can't put it down
How many CC's of morphine do they need?
I can't put it down
Hold his head still---but it's bloody
I can't put it down
HELP, HELP, don't just stand there, he's gonna die
I can't put it down
Where the fuck is the doctor.

"And I heard. It's okay honey, it's only falling dust! Breathe it out."

No matter how hard I push, try to throw it away,
I can't put it down. This ceiling fan sounds like a 'copter and often I'm sent into a trance.
Someone please save me from this disorder I'm stressed out, post-traumatically.

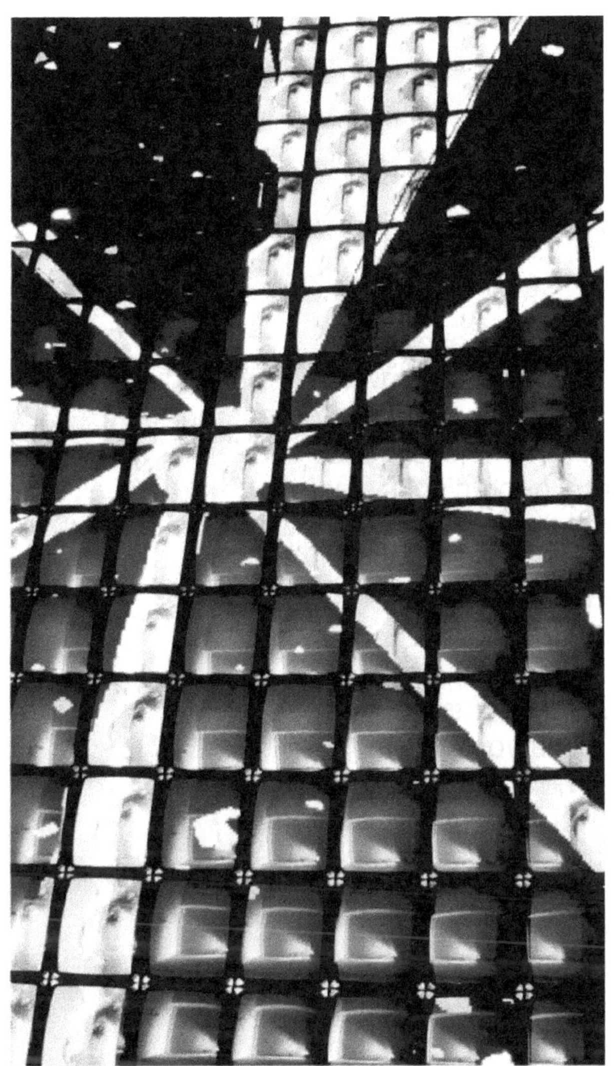

Television Holds

I'm Sleepy

Over here:
Ceiling fans and helicopter blades all look the same to me, when I lie in bed doped up on medication to fight my PTSD, all I want to do is get a good night sleep, but they are far and few between for me.

Over there:
Another shattered dream, and I mean that literally.
Awakened abruptly by the window pane shaking,
Vivid images in my head bursting together then
Falling apart mimicking smoke clouds and falling white blocks. All
I want to do is get a good night's sleep, but
Every night around three, the bombs start landing in flocks.

The night before the war:
Canada isn't that far from you.
Running is the practical thing to do.
Stop these running thoughts!
Eventually, they'll find you.
Tonight I need to get a good night's sleep,
Because tomorrow I leave for the war,
And it might be the last one for me.

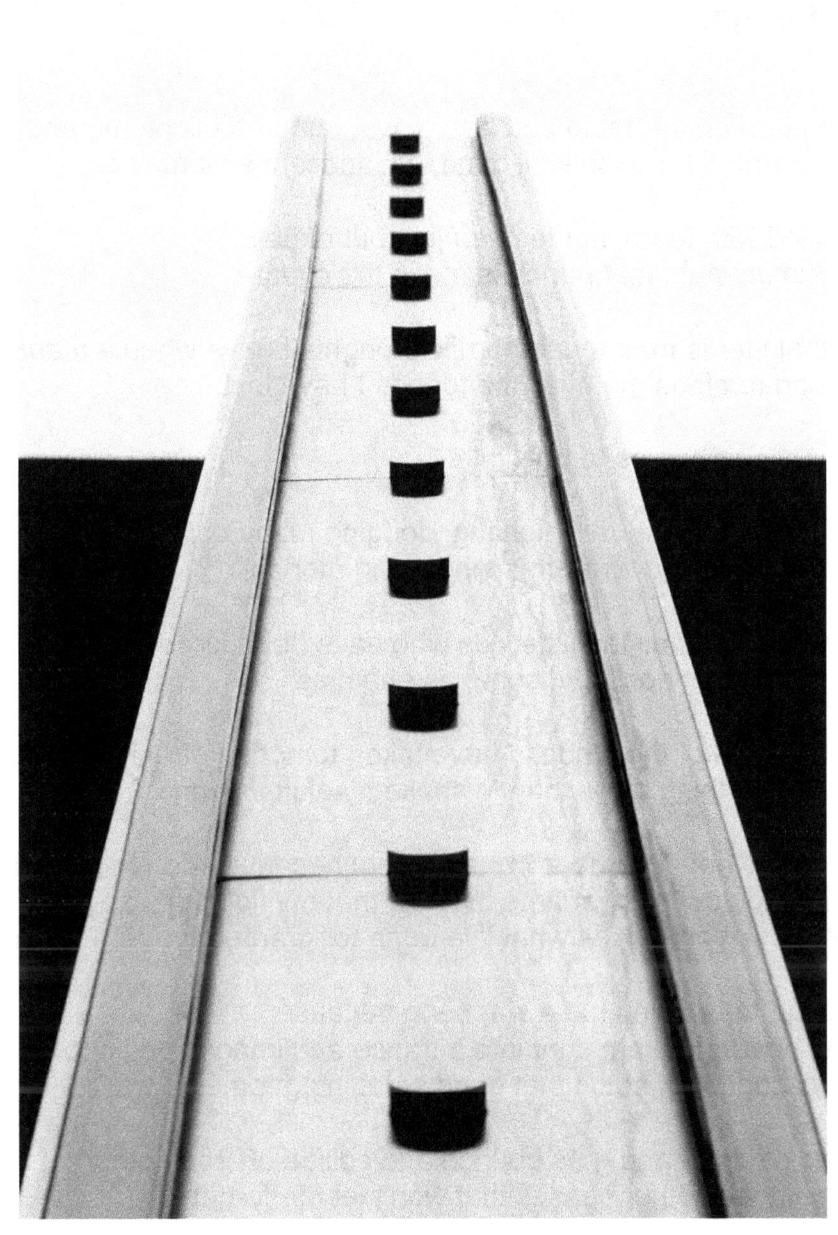

Moving Up!

War Songs

When I turn on the radio and hear a war song, thanking me and my fellow warriors for a job well done, as innocent as it may be,

I am filled with tears, not tears of joy, but of pain,
Excruciating pain that punches me in the chest.

Pain that stems from those horrific thoughts I have when a *thank you* war song reminds me of all the friends I have lost,

And my heart begins to palpitate.

I'm reminded of the daily fighting, dodging many bullets.
The ducking for cover from an incoming mortar.

It reminds me of all the little kids who have been killed,
Some of them innocently, some as enemies.

It reminds me of the strides I have taken to not be afraid of children, who want nothing more than to shake a soldier's hand.

I ask you to not sing me a war song, not because I don't appreciate it. I understand you just want me to know that my fighting was not in vain, and not everyone takes what I've done for granted.

I ask you, to not sing me a war song because,
when I hear one, I am sent into a trance and images begin to kaleidoscope, but not in that good amazing geometric way.

Images of blood and guts bounce and collide off each other awakening my other senses that won't let me forget:

The stench of charred flesh;

The way my comrades' body parts felt in my hands;

The way the dirt tasted when it splattered on my teeth after that I E D exploded and I was thrown to the dirt;

The screams of women, men, children, and my fellow soldiers alike.

I am not trying to put a damper on *thank you* war songs, but when I hear one

I find myself crying because I am filled with emotion that rips into my core as I am reminded of all the friends I have lost, and how powerless I was.

I'm reminded of the many men and women I've had to watch transition from this world into the next, offering comfort but nothing more.

I could not help them in their last hour.
I could do nothing about being sent to war.
I can't do anything about the tragedies that come along with war,

But I can ask you, to please not sing me another war song.

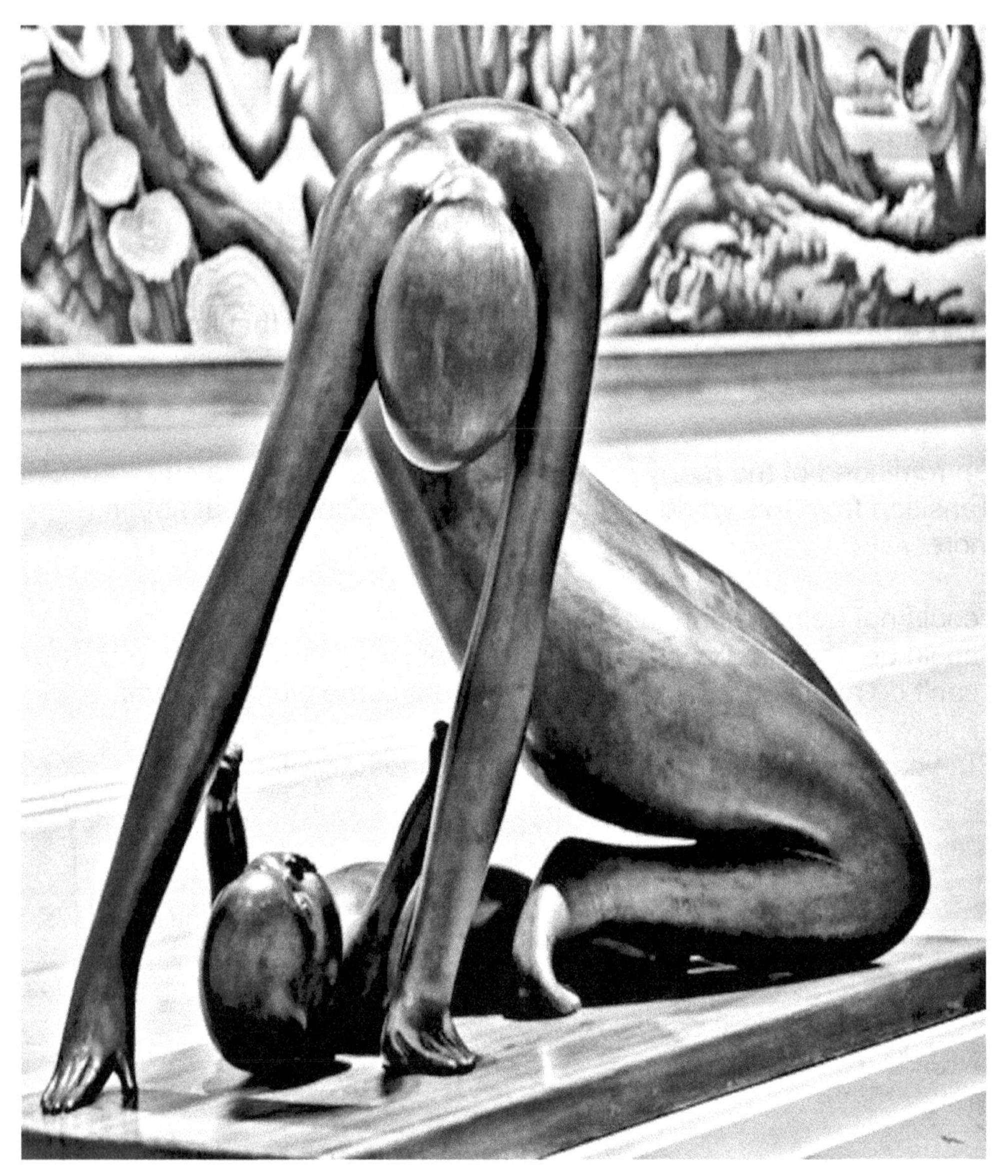

Forever

For You Someday For Helping Me Today

I want to thank you for helping see me through.
There will never be enough words of
gratitude.
It's people like you who make me proud
To have served in Iraq with a smile.

You have no idea how much you have helped me today.
Your kind gesture is forever marked in my heart and
goodness knows one day,
Although it may seem far away,
I'll return this favor in the most unexpected way.

Today, I may be homeless on the streets I
vowed to protect, haunted by images of the inhumane, but this fifty
cents you've given me,

I promise will go a long way.

TWO UNSUBSTANTIATED THEORIES

Sometimes I Get Lost In My Own Thoughts

Osho and Kush

If there were no ideomotor to which we adhere,
Would we feel the need to disappear?
Abandon the constraints of our lives because of fear?

I am asking a question about the combination of steps people take to follow the rules of doctrines and institutions, without understanding the nature of the actualized ideas. We do because we're told to. One person can come up with an idea, and people follow that person, eventually causing a movement. Sometimes, that one idea can have a dramatic effect on society as a whole, sometimes radicalizing small groups. Either way, after a while, it becomes something that people involuntarily or unconsciously follow, because someone before him has.

I'm questioning the astounding effects one person can have on society that everyone just goes along with, when we all have ulterior motives.

If people asked more questions instead of just involuntarily following the masses, and then trying to instill what they themselves don't understand onto others, would we live more peacefully and not always have to fight against the institutions we let govern us in the first place.

Language Evolution

Adding new words to an existing language, or dropping old ones is something people have always done. Language evolves just like living species, and if you think about it, it makes sense right. Well I have been thinking about a new phenomenon that is occurring right now around us, and want us all to be a participant. To sum it up--

It all starts with Bennifer – yes Bennifer the super couple or otherwise former pairing of Ben Affleck and Jennifer Lopez. Now when everyone hears Bennifer which, when said alone, is talking about the singular entity of Ben and Jen as a couple, the underlying inference is that you are talking about two distinct people: Ben Affleck and Jennifer Lopez. We have nationally, probably even globally, created, accepted, and now use the term Bennifer with fluency. So if we can take names and mesh them together like Kimye and Brangelina to make uni-names, why can't we do that with everyday words, to let's say explain how someone feels, or to describe two objects meshed together? Here are some examples to jump-start the word evolution movement. Try to come up with your own word (with a definition) that is true to the individual definitions of the portmanteau (WTH is that, you ask?), you have to Wikipedia it!

Irrastrated = Irritation + Frustration – to convey that one is feeling angry, provoked or annoyed while also being disappointed or thwarted.

Commosity = Commotion + Animosity – when a tumultuous motion, agitation, or noisy disturbance occurs triggered by a feeling of strong dislike or ill will.

Brookie = Brownie + Cookie- created when one mixes and bakes brownies and cookies together in a muffin pan. Found on Pinterest posted under DK Daniels/Just Desserts. Nena on Pinterest says ". . . 1 scoop of brownie batter + 1 scoop of cookie dough in a muffin pan...I call them brookies."

Cronut = Croissant + Donut - Described by many as a half croissant, half doughnut — this pastry hybrid by Chef Dominique Ansel is taking the world by storm.

A Short Story

The Waiting List

It's 6 a.m. and Felicity's alarm startles her. It does not wake her; it causes her to cry harder. She has been crying for the past two hours, as she does every morning. The alarm serves as a catalyst to the start of another sad day for Felicity.

Slowly she gets up and makes her way to the bathroom. The first thing she does is start filling the tub. For the past three years, ever since the acquittal, Felicity has filled the tub with cold water when she bathes.

She stares in the bathroom mirror, slowly wipes the tears from her eyes, and reads the note she has written herself. Try to smile today so people will leave you alone. After practicing a false smile, Felicity walks over and slowly slides into the tub, cringing at the coldness, but enjoying the pain, which eventually numbs her. The physical shock from the coldness eases the mental pain she has just for a second. It takes her mind off that fourteen-year-old boy.

Slowly she picks up the razor blade she's been staring at and flips it between her fingers. Yet again she is contemplating suicide, cutting her wrist or maybe stabbing herself in the neck with it, anything that would end her life.

The alarm in the kitchen goes off. It's 7 o'clock. She screams because it signals that she is still alive and must continue on. She slides underneath the water, hoping she will drown, but she knows she won't. She's too weak to kill herself.

Felicity slowly rises out of the tub and gets dressed for work, the only thing she leaves the house for. She must maintain until her number is pulled. The only thing that brings her joy is knowing that one day she will die.

A knock at the door startles her; no one ever visits except the grocery store delivery boy, and it's not Wednesday. Panic overwhelms Felicity as she slowly walks to the door, because she thinks a family member has found out where she is and is about to break her seclusion. She takes a deep breath and opens the door. No one is there. She drops her head and lets out a sigh of relief, and then she sees it. A black four-leaf clover.

Felicity has been waiting on this day for one year, four months, and seventeen days. Every second has mattered up until this point -- they matter from the moment your name is placed on the list. She picks up the clover, kisses it and screams for joy. She rushes into the living room, sits on the couch and kisses the piece of metal. She stomps her feet on the floor in a giddy manner before falling backward onto the couch. She takes in the moment, then starts repeating "three weeks, three weeks." She jumps up from the couch and calls her job to tell them she won't be back, ever.

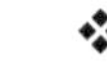

—

It's been four hours since Felicity found her clover and she is doing things she hasn't done in years. She is enjoying her environment. She is walking down the streets of her community, taking in the scent of the fresh air, feeling the flowers, petting the stray dog she has banished from her presence so many times before.

"It's a new day! I finally got my black clover," she says to the dog. Felicity spins around in the street a couple of times screaming, "whoo! I got the golden ticket."

She motions for the dog to follow her to the park. Felicity

and the dog spend hours frolicking, then a man approaches her. Someone she has never seen before, but she hardly ever noticed the local people anyway. He extends friendly conversation and she happily accepts; something she would not have done before this morning.

She only has three weeks to live and now this man comes into her life. It was three years ago that she left a party where she had three cocktails to celebrate the breakup from her boyfriend. The perfect way to blow off steam turned into her worst nightmare. After leaving the party at about 9 p.m., she ran across Matthew, a red-haired kid who was late for curfew. Trying to make his way home, he came out of no-where onto the busy road. People were screaming for him to stop, but he interpreted it as encouragement. He was in the middle of doing a failed feeble grind on his BMX bike, when he careened off of the rail onto the pavement in front of Felicity's car. Involuntary manslaughter is what she was charged with and she was placed on probation for four years.

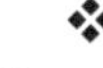

—

It's been sixteen days since Felicity received her clover. Life has changed drastically since she started enjoying life. She took the dog home with her and has been dating the guy, Irving, she met in the park. Her days of depression are behind her. She has begun to live again. Every morning, she looks forward to her day, and is in the shower before her 6 a.m. alarm. Her mind is free to wander and wonder about life again. Irving, her boyfriend, gives her hope for the future, so much so that she often forgets the fate she has signed up for. Her life is renewed and she wants to get off that damn list. But she can't. No one ever does. For two years, four months and seventeen days, all she thought about was death, but now she sees that she can be happy and regrets all the days she spent in a melancholy state.

Now she spends her days in the park and nights looking for shooting stars. On day seventeen, she decides she needs to tell Irving what is to come. She needs to start preparing for the inevitable and give him information to give her parents.

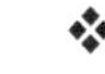

Felicity is writing out her will when Irving interrupts her thoughts by knocking on the door. She sits him on the couch and begins to slowly tell Irving about the list, why she put herself on a list to be killed and how, within five days, she will be gone.

"Irving, I need you to listen and try to not ask any questions okay. It's going to be a lot, what I'm about to tell you. I know you will have questions, but remember there is nothing that can change this situation. Three years ago, I killed a boy when I was driving home one night after a couple of drinks. They didn't send me to jail, and I became really depressed. After about a year, my doctor told me about this secret program, which I shouldn't even be telling you about, but I don't want you to wonder what happened to me. Anyway, there's this company out there that you can sign up to kill you, almost like assisted suicide, but there is a bunch of other stuff that goes along with it. So after you put yourself on the waiting list, an assassin brings you this clover to let you know you have three weeks left to live."

Irving tries to interrupt. She places her hand on his knee, "Please let me finish. You never know when you're going to get your black four-leaf clover, it just shows up one day to let you

know that anytime within the next three weeks they will kill you or snatch you for research."

As she tries to explain how she regrets her decision, Irving gets up and walks to the kitchen to get glasses of water for them. He is taken back by her confession; he has never encountered a situation like this before, someone confessing like this.

Before going back to sit down, he starts to down the glass of water he poured for himself.

"You don't have to bring it to me; I'll come in the kitchen with you. I need to move around."

"Are you sure?" He asks. She says, "yes."

While getting up off of the couch, she trips over the bag Irving has left by the table. She leans over to pick the things up that have fallen out. For a moment she pauses, then picks up one of the four- leaf clovers that have fallen out of a small pouch. She gasps, causing Irving to look in her direction.

"It's time, Felicity. I'm sorry," Irving says in a solemn voice.

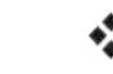

It's 6 a.m. and Felicity's alarm signals to Irving that it's time for him to leave. He's not done cleaning yet, and the delivery boy will be there soon. He tunes the alarm out and hurriedly tries to erase his presence. He's been here too long, way too long; he cared too much for her. He has been faltering lately, getting too close. With each new job, his heart softens for his clients. He does not know how much longer he will be able to continues this. But he must get out soon, and he must leave this gloomy apartment before it's too late. Irving feeds the dog, wipes down the last glass he used, then the doorknob before disappearing down the hallway. He sighs. "On to the next job. Time is ticking... it is always ticking away."

About the Author

Boy were the stars aligned lopsided when they birthed me.

Celestially a Leo, biologically a Virgo. Rushing to enter this
world too soon, and I've been running ever since.
Jumping over every hurdle imaginable,
Sometimes wanting to end the race too soon,

But then things escaped the grasps of spatial starry omegas, and the one true supernatural being took over and is now guiding me through. Slowing my stride, taking me by the hand, and amazingly the hurdles are disappearing, and by God, now I can actually see a happy ending to this melancholic dream.

Erika Land spent most of her military career serving as a Pharmacy Technician states-side with a one-year deployment to Mosul, Iraq between the years 2005 and 2006. Her initial plan was to attend pharmacy school, but along the way she realized her passion for writing. Erika's first novel, Misconceptions, of the book series "It's Complicated" was a passion project that has evolved into a full-blown writing career. Writing also serves as a therapeutic measure for Erika, because it helps her deal with her Post Traumatic Stress Disorder. Erika's perspective of life is "It's not going to hurt me to help, so why not", which has prompted her to do a lot of the volunteer work she does now. Find out more information about her www.erikarland.com

About the Photographer

KaTisha Smittick, a retired US Army Staff Sergeant, works as a freelance photographer in the Washington D.C. area. She is known to travel all over the world to seek out new and exciting subjects to capture and share with her audience. KaTisha thrives by being in the middle of all the chaos of the world then turning that into inspiring photos. KaTisha photographs a wide variety of charity venues, events, and shows. Her work has been published online, in print and has been featured on clients' websites and promotional materials. Her outlook on being a photographer is summed up in a personal motto of hers, "Dedication to what you believe in just isn't enough, but living in it will show you what you are made of."

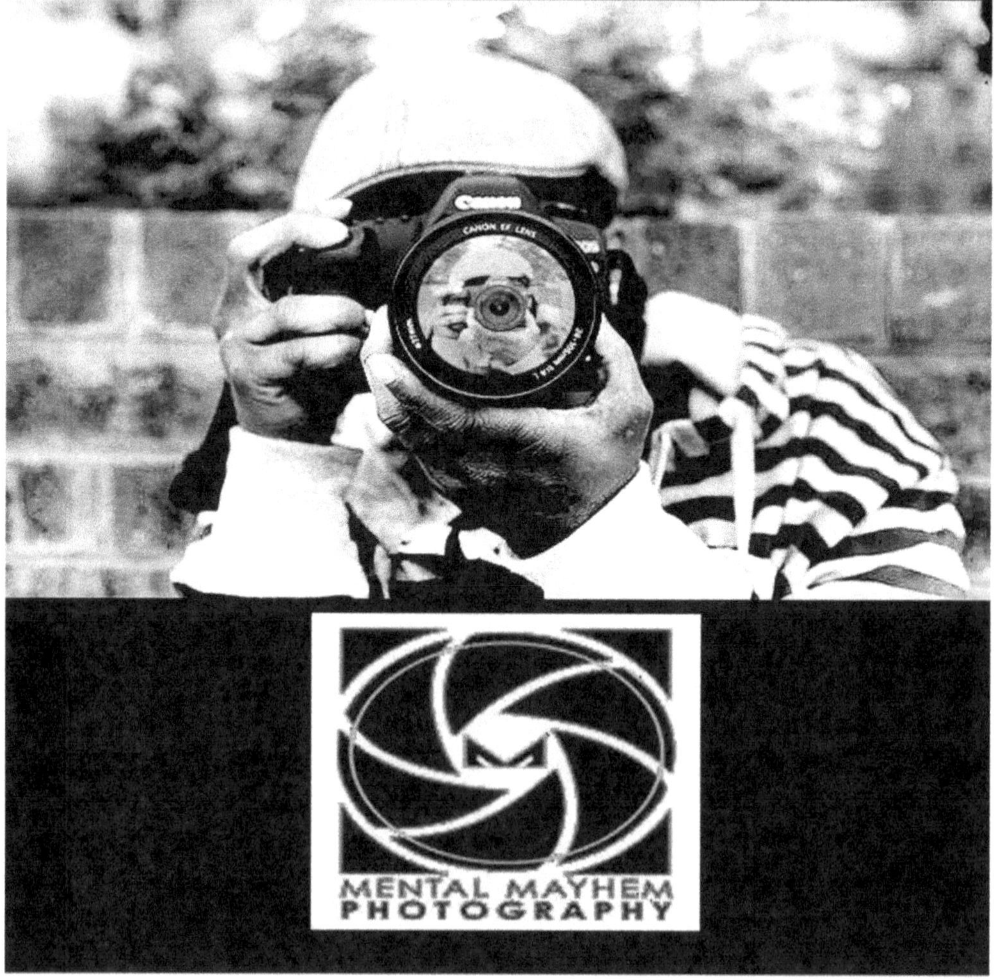

www.ingramcontent.com/pod-product-compliance
Lightning Source LLC
LaVergne TN
LVHW011628120826
845149LV00022B/2757